This story belongs to:

_____

BIG MO

For Alex,
Happy reading! I
hope you will LOVE Mo ☺

2015

For the little Padaleckis, **BIG** and small
- Aunt Meggie

Library of Congress Control Number | 2014920253

Publisher's Cataloging-in-Publication
(Provided by Quality Books, Inc.):

Padalecki, Megan, author, artist.
Big Mo / story & pictures by Megan Padalecki.
pages cm
Summary | When Mo's appetite gets out of hand, he grows too large for his home, only to discover that he was full all along.
Audience | Ages 4-8.
ISBN 978-0-692-32711-1

1. Iguanas as pets -- Juvenile fiction. 2. Body size -- Juvenile fiction.
3. Stories in rhyme. [1. Iguanas as pets -- Fiction. 2. Size -- Fiction.
3. Stories in rhyme.] I. Title

PZ8.3.P126Bi 2014   [E]
QBI14-2144

Printed and bound in the United States of America
First Edition | December 2014
10 9 8 7 6 5 4 3 2 1

www.padaleckistudio.com

BIG MO

Story and Pictures by
MEGAN PADALECKI

VERY HUNGRY
IGUANA
(FREE TO good HOME!)

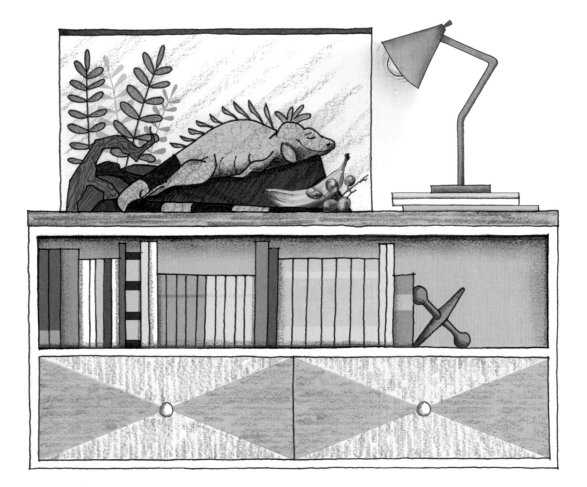

Mo came home that first day with a grin on his face,

"Things to eat and free heat?! What a *wonderful* place!"

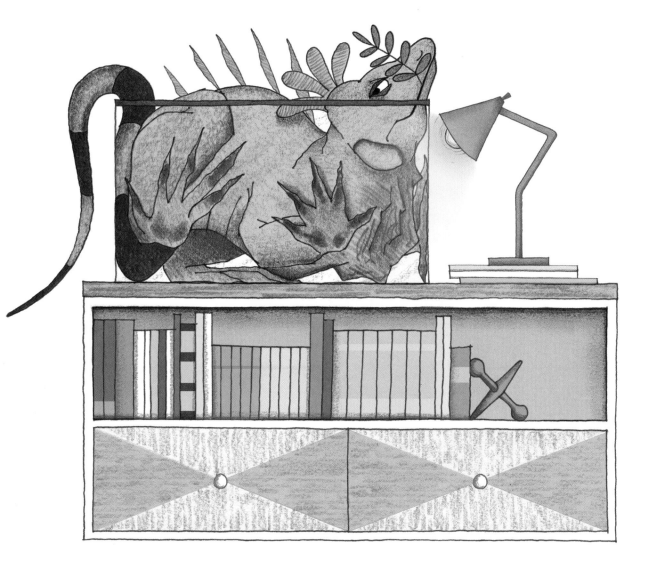

But he must have been hungry, or *famished*, or WORSE,

When he started a frenzy he could not reverse!

Things could get out of hand when he put his mind to it —
Mo swallowed his tank as he quickly outgrew it!

He burst through the wall
And he did not stop there –
He eyeballed *more* snacks
As he crawled down the stair.

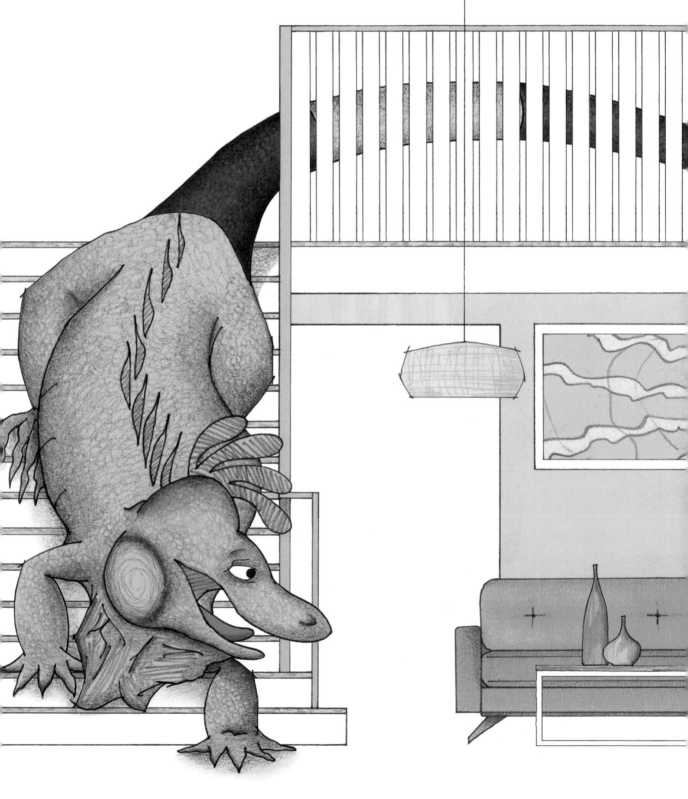

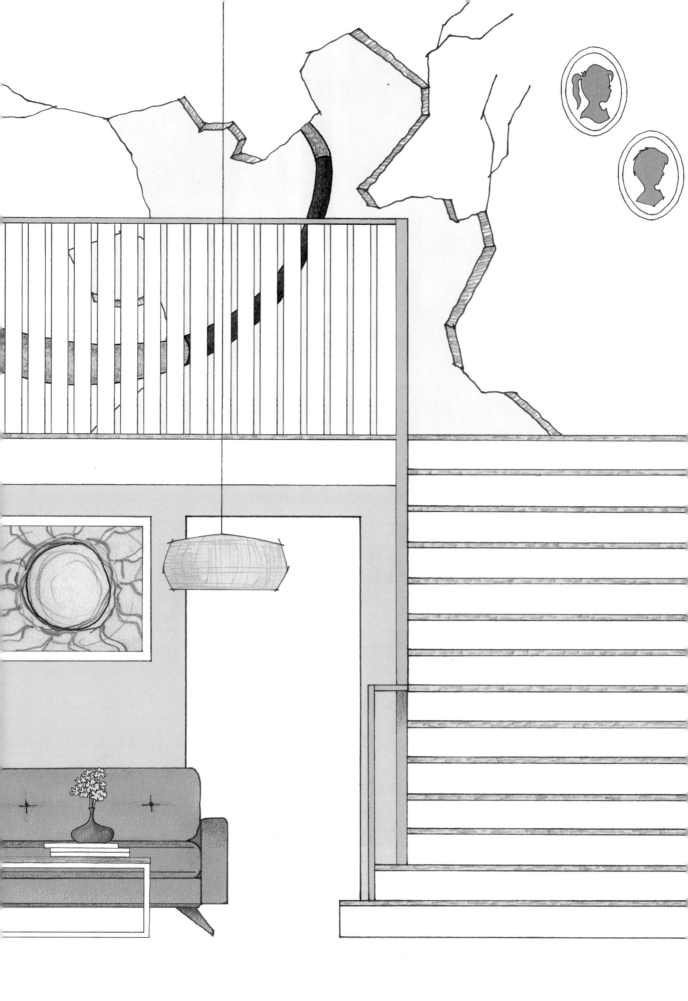

Mo noticed his house felt a little too **tight** –

There was nothing too large

Just to **chomp**

In one bite!

This meal would set records!
Make headlines galore:

"Iguana Shocks World As
He Eats More and More!"

They'd call him a **menace!**
A **monster!**
A **threat!**

Whoever would guess he was once just a pet?

Mo dragged his big belly and tail through the woods –
Ate cedars and spruces, and lush neighborhoods.

Then he climbed on a rock just to rest for a while...

...But he quickly returned to his feast with a smile.

He could not get enough!
He reached up to the sky!
He was gorging and growing without asking why.

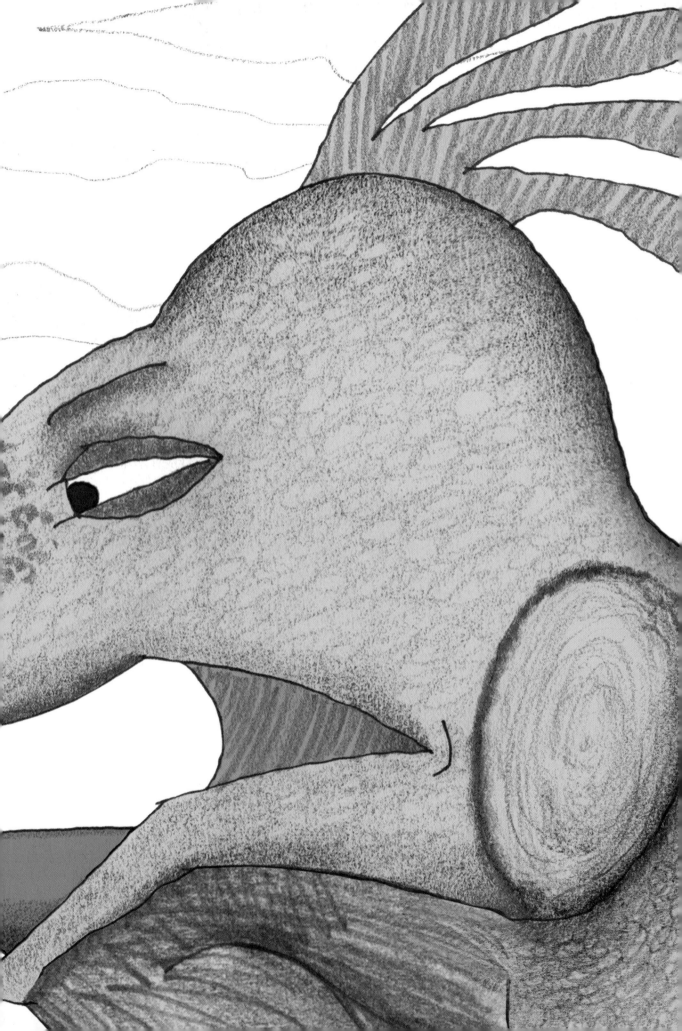

When the clouds were devoured, Mo sunk to the sea –
If *new* snacks were cooking, then that's where he'd be!

Mo's choices for chewing were fewer by now.

He should have just stopped, but he didn't know how.

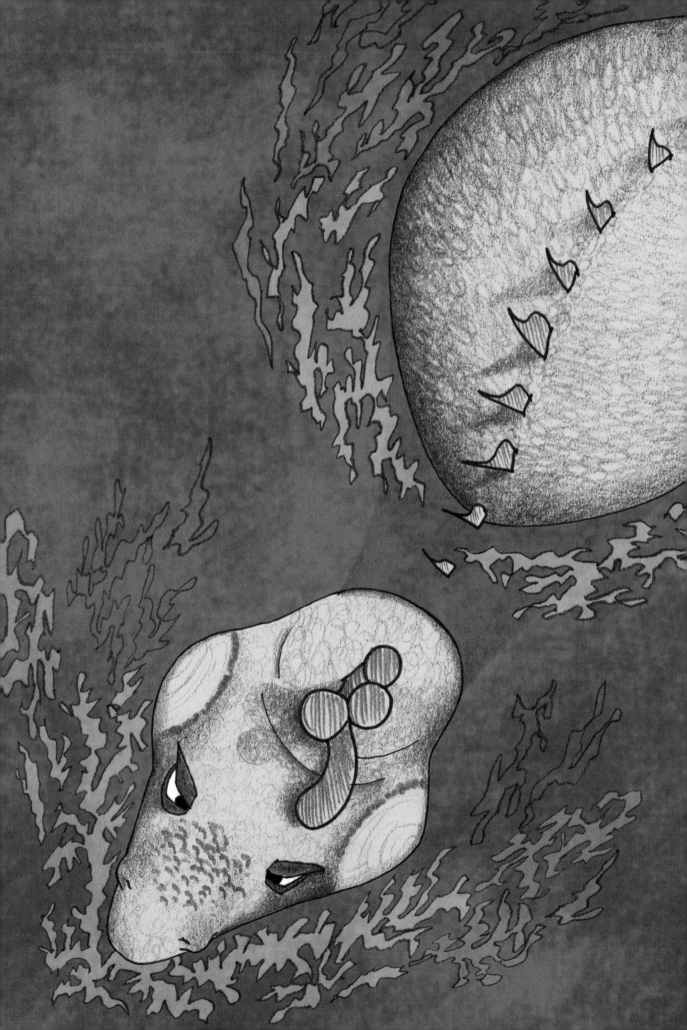

Moving slowly from weight
Far too great to support,
Mo guzzled the seas
As his final resort.

But then Mo saw nothing – was cold and alone.
The darkness around him chilled right to the bone.

Something seemed *off*,
But he just could not quit...

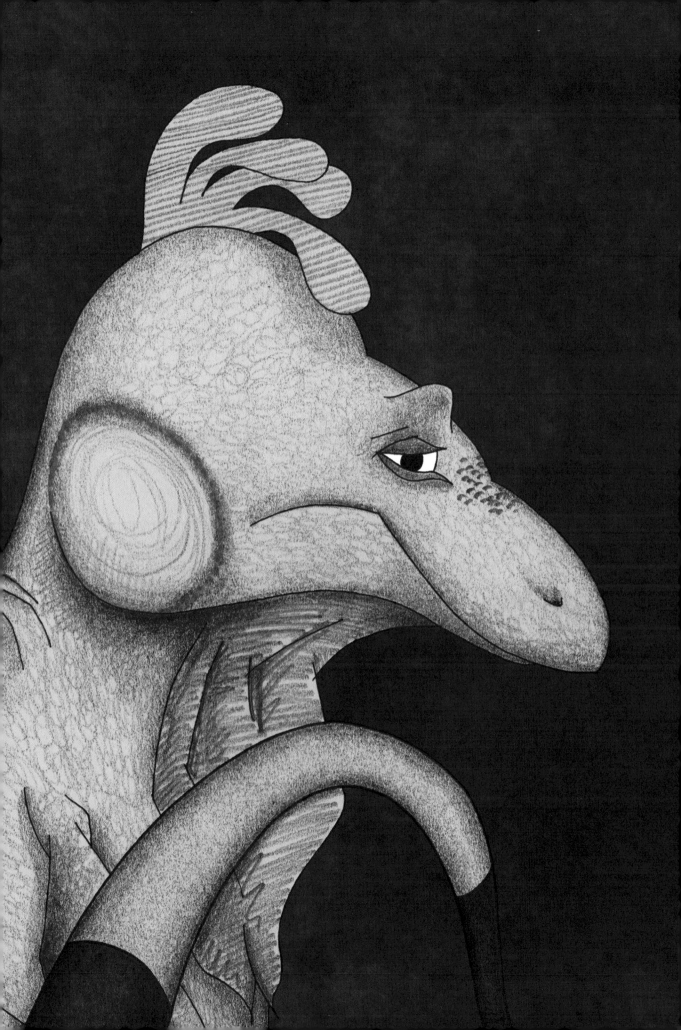

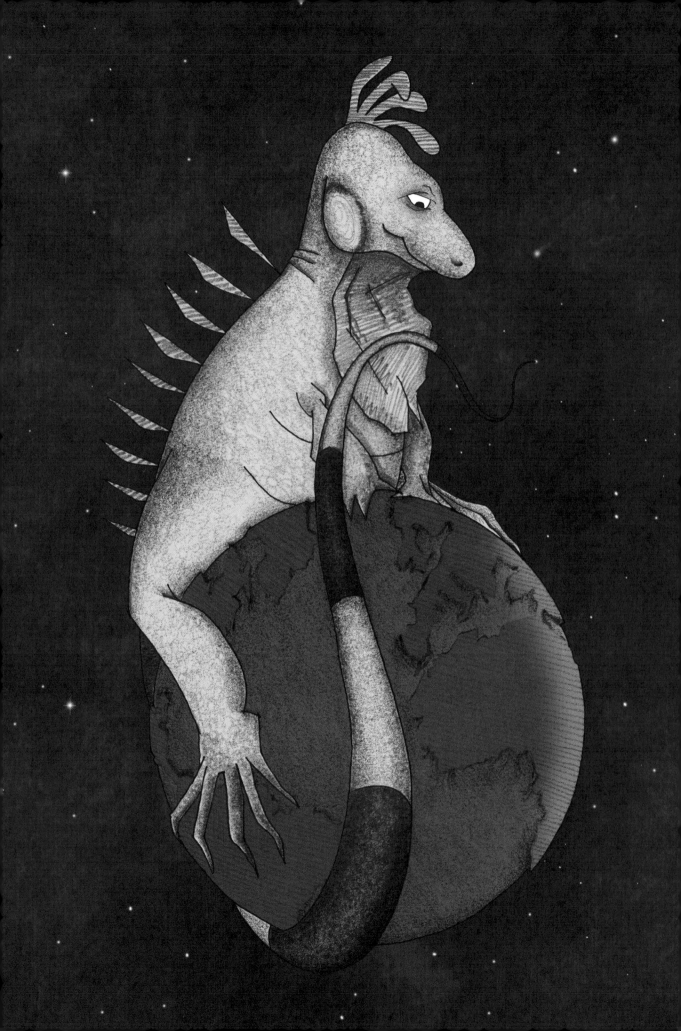

...Big Mo was not full without

every

last

bit.

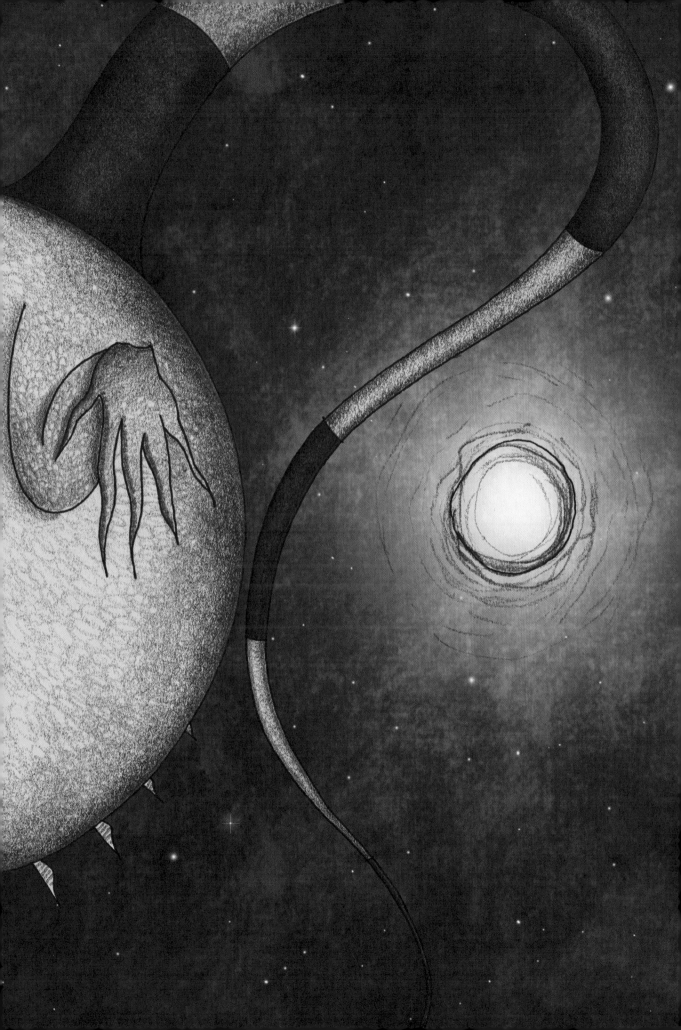

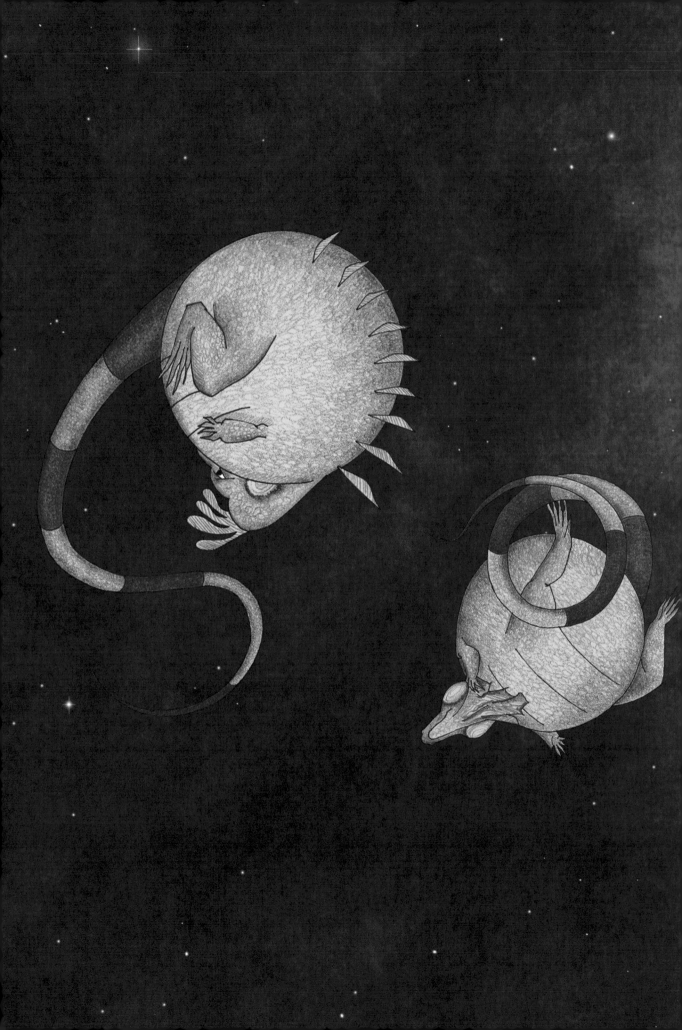

Mo floated along and at last he could see,

"I have taken the things meant for all, just for me."

Still, something familiar grew brighter and near –
It warmed Mo right up, and it eased all his fear!

He awoke with surprise and relief, "It's all here!"
And he beamed at his lamp, which beamed back,
Bright and clear.

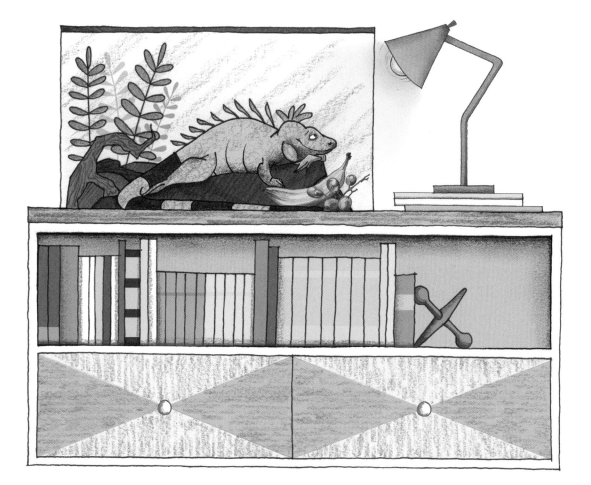

His home now seemed precious and Mo had a hunch
He'd be perfectly full when he finished his lunch.

About this book

The illustrations for this book were hand-drawn in ink, rendered in 2B pencil, and digitally colored and composed.

This book was edited by Megan, Jared, Sharon and Veronique Padalecki. Contributors were Ryan Golenberg and Robert Remar, and a group of the author's trusted fellow architects and designers. This is the author's first book.

Text was set in Museo Sans, and display type was set in League Spartan. The story was printed on 70 lb Husky Woodfree paper with 95% opacity.